BLUFF

D0626259

WINE

HARRY EYRES

RAVETTE BOOKS

Published by Ravette Books Limited
3 Glenside Estate, Star Road
Partridge Green, Horsham,
West Sussex RH13 8RA
(0403) 710392

First printed 1987
Reprinted 1989, 1991
Revised 1992

Series Editor - Anne Tauté

Cover design - Jim Wire
Printing & Binding - Cox & Wyman Ltd.
Production - Oval Projects Ltd.

The Bluffer's Guides are based on
an original idea by Peter Wolfe.

CONTENTS

INTRODUCTION

Wine attracts mystique like no other drink and few other subjects. Many people are defeated by wine thinking that in order to claim any knowledge of it they need:

a to have visited various vineyards in France
b) to have a cellar (i.e. not a cupboard under the stairs), or
c) to be able to identify exactly where a wine comes from without looking at the label.

This, needless to say, is nonsense. Gone are the days when the wine drinker would ignore anything that didn't come from France, Germany, Spain (only sherry of course) or Portugal (vintage port). Upstarts from the New World like California and Australia have put themselves firmly on the map; sleeping giants like Italy and Spain are waking up; even the most unlikely newcomers like Bulgaria have appeared and surprised everybody with their quality. The message to the bluffer, then, is not to be intimidated by the mystique.

Some knowledge of the old traditions and etiquette is desirable, however, so that you can take on the wine bore at his own game and win. It is no longer safe, alas, to follow Stephen Potter's inspired advice to confine yourself to completely meaningless remarks like 'too many tramlines'.

This guide sets out to conduct you through the main danger zones: places and circumstances in which you are most likely to encounter wine and the wine expert, and to equip you with a vocabulary and an evasive technique that will minimise the risk of your being found out.

THE BASICS

What is Wine?

There is no argument about this, wine is fermented grape juice. People may make, drink and even talk about elderflower wine, peach wine, kiwi-fruit wine or whatever, but you do not need to know about them. You should even avoid drinking them. On no account discuss them. They have no mystique and thus no bluffing potential. Non-alcoholic wines are not wines. Wines, like some human beings, have an absolute need to be alcoholic.

The Three Colours

The next most important thing about wine is that it comes in three colours:

Red – which ranges from purple to light brown

White – which is usually pale yellow

Rosé – which is to be avoided (unless it comes from Navarra).

Sweet and Dry

First it as well to remember that anything calling itself medium is in fact **sweet**. Second, all wines, (except those made from grapes affected by the noble rot) are naturally **dry**. The sweetness comes either from stopping the fermentation before all the sugar has been converted to alcohol, or from adding unfermented grape-juice, or from adding sugar, usually in

6

liquid form.

All this does not mean that you should scorn sweet wines. The ignorant have turned their noses up at them for so long that a very rewarding bluffing line can be cultivated in, say, the little-known sweet white wines of the Loire, or the really fine German Auslesen, Beerenauslesen, and Trockenbeerenauslesen. It is relief to know that the last two can be shortened to BA and TBA. If you want to create a frisson, recommend an Austrian TBA from a place called Rust.

Fortification

Most wines are unfortified, that is to say they have only the alcohol provided by God in the form of sun and grapes (plus sugar beet in the 'must' if they are French). But some wines, like port, sherry, madeira and the two venerable old white wines, marsala and malaga, are strengthened by the addition of anything from brandy to industrial alcohol. Fortified wines, like fortified towns, are not to be taken lightly. They get you buzzing more quickly but land you up with the most appalling after-effects if you're not careful.

Still and Sparkling

This should be self-explanatory. Wines either come in thick heavy bottles with corks wrapped round with wire which are impossible to get out, in which case they are **sparkling** (i.e. fizzy, but for some reason this word must not be used of wines) or, in ordinary bottles with ordinary corks, which are impossible to get out, in which case they are **still**.

7

The fun begins when you discover that many still wines are slightly fizzy, or rather, sparkling. Sometimes this is intentional, as with vinho verde. Even when it is not intentional, this is not necessarily considered a fault. The thing to do, in any case, is to say "Hmm... slightly pétillant" (if it's French) or "Possibly spritzig" (if it's German).

Essential Equipment

Unless you can pass yourself off as a wine writer, cash is indispensable. Unlike some other art-forms, wine has to be bought and consumed to be appreciated. There are, however, a few other essentials:

1. Nose

Ninety per cent of the taste of a wine is perceived via the nose. You will appreciate this if you have a bad cold. The most famous nose in the wine business is possessed by Don José Ignacio Domecq of the well known sherry firm: this is long and beaky and fits conveniently inside the small, tapered sherry glasses called copitas. It is probably a case of natural selection. Non-sherry tasters do not need such an impressive proboscis, but the equipment inside it must be operative.

2. Corkscrew

Decent wine comes in bottles with corks for which, unfortunately, no really satisfactory device for extraction has yet been invented. One can understand why, in the old days, choleric gentlemen used to decapitate bottles with red-hot pincers, but this is sadly out of fashion, and in any case difficult without a blazing fire. You should probably opt for the 'waiter's friend' or the screwpull. But if someone praises the latter too fulsomely you can murmur "Ah, but wait until the non-stick coating wears out."

Types of corkscrew to be avoided include the bulbous Russian doll variety (you can't see what you're doing with it and the handle tends to come off mid-screw), the double-armed ratchet type (which has a drill-like action that can bore a hole through the cork, and it catches your fingers in its ratchets), or the vacuum variety which pumps the air out. This can blow up the bottle.

Go for the simplest kind so long as it has a good wire worm screw and a comfortable, firmly attached handle. This has good inverted bluffing potential and the great advantage of working.

3. Glasses

It is generally agreed that wine should be drunk from a glass, though for the desperate, any water-tight receptacle will do. Glasses have the advantage of not affecting the flavour as leather bottles, metal goblets and old boots do. You can also see what you're drinking.

The kind of glass is relatively unimportant, though a tulip shape, which gathers the **bouquet** (see Smell) is considered best for most wines. Otherwise, the simpler the better.

5. Decanters

These are strictly unnecessary, except for old red

wines and vintage and crusted ports which have muck in the bottom of the bottle. No one can decide whether or not one should decant burgundy. Decanting, apart from separating the wine from the muck, exposes it to the atmosphere and therefore lets it breathe. Some wines, however, especially very old ones, do not take well to the atmosphere and fade away. Decanting very old wines, therefore, is a risky business.

White wines, including sherry, should not be decanted. It is unnecessary, and indeed harmful to the wine, and besides, the effect will be unpleasantly medical (perhaps another reason why white wine is usually put in green bottles). On the other hand by all means decant an inexpensive port if you want to pass it off as vintage.

Decanting is the process of pouring the contents into a decanter and stopping before the muck gets in. It sounds easy. It is easy. But it must be made to look as difficult as possible. The aim is to make the performance resemble a Black Mass. A candle must be used, supposedly to show when the sediment reaches the neck, but in fact to induce ceremonial atmosphere. Absolute silence must be observed and a look of rapt concentration maintained, until the last drop of clear liquid has been transferred.

After this, a dramatic sigh, wipe of the brow and momentary indication of emotional exhaustion, as of an actor having just played a great tragic role, may be called for to underline the risk involved. It is particularly important to sniff the cork of the bottle being decanted: it may then be attached to the neck of the decanter. This is roughly equivalent to the handing back to the patient of an organ which has been surgically removed.

6. Cellar and Storage

Bluffers should not be afraid to talk about their cellar even if they do not possess anything remotely approximating an underground storeroom. A cellar for these purposes is a collection of at least two bottles, or possibly a single bottle, of reasonable quality. If you are keeping wine for any length of time, however, there are two important rules to observe.

1. To avoid the corks drying out and letting air in, bottles should be kept lying down (on their side) or better still, upside down. This will look impressively eccentric, but is in fact the normal way for bottles to lie when being transported or stored.

2. Wine should be kept somewhere with a reasonably constant temperature, preferably not above 60°F (a fairly cool day). This is likely to be impossible to achieve, in which case remember a constant temperature of 70°F is better than a fluctuation between 40°F and 60°F. Or simply drink your wine quickly before it has a chance to go off.

Poor cellaring conditions have one advantage, namely that wine will mature more quickly in them. Certain Bordeaux vintages which have taken ages to come round (1970, 1975) might be greatly improved by a spell in a centrally heated flat.

7. Serving Temperature

The concern about serving wine at the right temperature can lead people to extreme measures like baking claret in the oven or icing Sauternes. These are probably inadvisable, though wine is surprisingly resilient.

11

The rule is that most red wines should be served at room temperature (the French term is 'chambré') and most white wines lightly chilled, i.e. having spent an hour in the fridge or twelve minutes in the freezer. Snobs tend to be suspicious of the freezer which suggests that they once forgot to take wine out of it.

There is an intermediate state between chilled and chambré, namely cellar temperature. This is a very useful category, because it can mean the temperature the wine happens to be when you have forgotten to chill or warm it. Some light red wines like Beaujolais are best quaffed at this temperature anyway. If a red wine is too cold, you can suggest your guests warm it by cupping the glass in their hands. Use the French 'châleur de la main' to add further refinement.

History

The history of wine is very long and involved, stretching back as it does to way before Roman times. Mercifully you need deal only with the last one hundred years because the vines in Europe, Africa, and very nearly everywhere else, were all but wiped out by a plague of aphides. This affliction, *phylloxera vastatrix*, attacked and destroyed the roots of the vines. Fortunately for us it took nearly 30 years to do so. During that time wine growers had a chance to import native vinestocks from the United States, and graft what remained of the famous grape varieties on to them.

It may still be possible to find a doddering ancient who can remember the last bottle of pre-phylloxera wine. But unless you are a grey-bearded loon of phenomenal age there is no point in your trying this.

TASTING AND DRINKING

Bluffers should never forget that tasting and drinking are two distinct activities and should not be confused.

Tasting is an unpleasant professional activity which people do to earn a living. It is done standing up. It involves rude noises, wry faces and spittoons.

Tasters *never* swallow. Well, hardly ever. One man in a pinstripe suit at a smart London tasting was heard asking another, 'What do you think of the Niederhäuser Hermannshöhle Spätlese 1985?' The other man paused judiciously before replying, 'I honestly don't know, but it slips down a treat'.

Drinking, on the other hand, is pleasure. It is done sitting down, except at drinks parties, which are in any case seldom a pleasure. It is true that if you are drinking decent wine, you should go through some of the motions of tasting, but you will do so in a different spirit.

The motions of tasting are the following:

1. Pour out a little wine, filling the glass no more than a quarter full. Stare fixedly at it. Look mean. If it is red, tilt the glass and hold it against a white surface. Yours not to question why.

2. Hold the glass firmly by the base and twirl it round either clockwise or anti-clockwise, but not both at the same time. Twirling does require a little practice: too vigorous a twirl will send the wine sloshing over the edge, too little vigour will have no effect on the wine. The theory is that it releases the bouquet. In fact, it proves that you are a pro.

13

3. Having twirled, sniff. Here an impressively shaped nose undoubtedly helps. Blocked sinuses do not. Some people favour moving the nose from side to side over the wine, presumably to give each nostril its share, but this can look rather sinister.

4. Only after these preliminaries is it permissible to take liquid into your mouth. A fairly large sip, in contrast to the small measure in the glass, is the thing, but not too large to enable you to perform the most difficult trick, which is to take in a small amount of air with an audible sucking noise at the same time as the wine. This is supposed to aerate the wine in your mouth and release more flavour. It is not the same as gargling. Try to avoid gargling – unless you have a sore throat. Wine, after all, is an antiseptic.

5. Having swilled it about a bit, spit the wine out as elegantly as possible into a spittoon, box of saw-dust or potted plant. There is a marked spitting order at some tastings. Watch out for this or you will get indelible young claret upon your front. Mind you, it is very easy to put it there yourself.

6. Surreptitiously drink some of the wine you liked best.

7. Take notes on all stages except (6).

When drinking a good wine, or one that your host considers good, limit yourself to tilting, twirling and sniffing. Do these things in a gracious, smiling manner, rather than with the fixed, suspicious glare of the professional taster. Do not try to take in air with the wine. You may not be asked again.

A drinker should not fill his glass more than half full if he is going to attempt twirling. He may feel that this is too great a sacrifice.

Talking about Wine

For some reason, many people feel that drinking, or even tasting and drinking, wine is not enough: they must also talk about it. Indeed social gatherings among the wine-loving fraternity seem to revolve almost solely around talk about wine. You may secretly find this boring or pretentious, but clearly as a bluffer you need not only to be able to drink and taste wine properly but also to hold up your end in wine-speak.

This is a complicated subject, but a few simple rules can get you a surprisingly long way.

1. Do not use words except where strictly necessary. Noises either non-committal ('Hmmm....') or enthusiastic ('Mmm.... Aah!') and facial contortions (raised eyebrows, narrowed glance, pursed lips) are often adequate, and do not commit you to anything.

2. The word 'Yes' is quite sufficient in most cases. It can be said in an infinite variety of tones – doubtful, quizzical, interrogative, tentative, affirmative, decisive, appreciative, enthusiastic, ecstatic. It can be repeated, in a clipped, conversation-stopping

manner ('Yes. Yes.'), or in a rising, excited tone ('Yesyesyes!').

3. Put off describing what the wine actually tastes like for as long as possible. Limit yourself to some of the following technical expressions as far as you can.

   a) Mention **ullage**. This means the level of wine in the bottle. If you have noticed that the bottle is not completely full, say in a neutral tone 'Ah, slightly ullaged'. It could be, of course, that your host has swigged some of it beforehand.

   b) Ask whether the wine has 'thrown a **deposit**'. Deposit of course, refers to the muck in the bottom of the bottle, not to what you get back when you return the empties to the off-licence.

   c) If it's a red wine, and you have noticed when tilting it that it leaves a thick transparent trail on the glass (most red wines do), say that it has 'good legs'.

Appearance

When you have exhausted these gambits, talk about the colour. You are on fairly safe ground here unless you are colour-blind, since it is easier to describe visual phenomena than tastes or smells. It might be a good idea to mug up your metals and semi-precious stones: different shades of gold, amber, garnet, ruby etc. seem to go down particularly well.

Smell

When talking about smell, do not use the word 'smell'. In English this usually has unpleasant connotations. Choose instead from **nose** (which with wine does not have unpleasant associations), **aroma** or **bouquet**, if you're feeling flowery.

If the wine doesn't smell of anything, and you know you do not have a cold, try 'Rather dumb on the nose, don't you find?' or 'Still very closed-up.'

Alternatively, if it smells very strongly, you can say, 'It's very forward on the nose'. None of these comments, of course, commits you to an opinion of the wine's quality.

If you have to become more specific, here are some of the more commonly used 'nose' words:

oaky, buttery, vanilla-ey – all used, interchangeably it seems, to describe certain wines which spend a considerable time in oak barrels, especially red Rioja and white Burgundy and its Californian and Australian clones.

blackcurranty – only use when you have checked that the wine is made from the Cabernet Sauvignon grape.

spicy – only used when you know that the wine is made from the Gewurztraminer grape. This is a very vague term considering how many different spices there are, but such things do not worry the cognoscenti.

Of course, people will say wines smell of anything; violets, truffles (either the kind pigs dig up in

Perigord or the delicious dusted chocolate balls), beet-roots, sweaty saddles, wet socks, farmyards, petrol (used of old Rieslings, which can have a curious oily whiff, and best said, like so many things, in French – 'goût de pétrole').

Smells are oddly evocative, but often these corre-spondences seem entirely personal and do not work for others. There is nothing to stop you trying this kind of thing, the more personal the better, because it cannot then be disproved. For instance, "This wine reminds me of one evening I spent in Crete. I don't know exactly what the connection is – the wild thyme, the sea-air, the flock of goats in the distance..."

Describing Wine

It is a truth universally acknowledged that there are few words to describe tastes – sweet, dry, acid are simply not enough. There isn't even a generally agreed word for the opposite of acid, and it is doubtful whether there are other definitive words to describe the taste of wine, since few wines are either salty or bitter enough for those two other unmistakable qualities to come into play. All the rest is metaphor – a poet's dream, but a bluffer's nightmare. Before you despair, quite a lot of mileage can be got out of the three main words.

Sweet and Dry

Degrees of sweetness and dryness are perhaps on the obvious side, but in wine-speak there is no harm in stating the obvious. It is particularly useful if you know how sweet or how dry a wine is meant to be, and then can suggest that it somehow contradicts expectations. Thus, "Surprisingly dry for a Sauternes/ Beerenauslese" or "This Chablis isn't as bone dry as I would have expected" are effective because they show others that:

(a) you know your stuff

(b) you have original, even if wrong, opinions.

Almost all red wines, incidentally, are dry. There is not much point in saying that a claret (burgundy) is dry; if you try to be original and opine that your host's Château Lafite is surprisingly sweet, you may not be given a second glass.

Acid

You can get further by talking about acidity. Acidity in wine, funnily enough, is generally considered a good thing, and so the comment 'Good acidity' can work wonders. This is especially true of white wines, in which acidity is synonymous with freshness. A white wine with too little acidity can be criticised for being heavy, flat or simply fat (see Body).

Wines can, of course, be too acid. This tends to be a fault of wines from cold countries and regions like Germany, Champagne and England. Comments on excess acidity are often expressed in involuntary, physical forms.

Wine, without getting too technical, contains different kinds of acidity. The best kinds, tartaric and lactic for instance, do not have a pronounced taste but impart freshness (or zinginess) to the wine. There are other kinds of acidity which do have a marked taste: malic acid makes wine taste like apples, not necessarily a bad thing. 'Appley' is good word to use of Mosel wines, for instance. The worst kind of acidity is acetic, also known as vinegar. If you think a wine tastes vinegary, but don't want to upset your host, say, "This wine has rather high volatile acidity, don't you think?" It isn't considered nearly so rude.

Balance

Even good acidity on its own is not enough: a wine needs to be balanced. **Balance** is perhaps the key concept in the wine world. Fortunately nobody ever asks exactly what is balanced with what: the idea is that all the constituent parts of a wine, alcohol, acidity fruit, are roughly in harmony.

Unlike unbalanced people, unbalanced wines do not do unpredictable things: in fact they are usually very ordinary. A perfectly balanced wine is a rare and wonderful thing.

Tannin

Here is a more friendly term for the bluffer. Tannin is a preservative substance extracted from the grape skins, pips and stems, mainly found in red wines. It is easily recognisable because it grips the back of your teeth, rather like those little sucker things the dentist puts in your mouth. Like the dentist, tannin leaves your teeth in need of the services of a hygienist. Young red wines which are the opposite of mellow are likely to be tannic.

Hard and **tannic** are two adjectives which commonly go together, particularly when you are tasting young claret, one of the most unpleasant of all aesthetic experiences. If you are given a claret and find it about as attractive and yielding as a Scottish bank manager, you may say "Still rather tannic, I find." There is a danger here: some wines (especially clarets) like some bank managers, no doubt, pass from being unpleasantly hard and tannic (i.e. too young) to being unpleasantly 'dried out' (i.e. too old) without any intervening stage of pleasant mellowness.

Fruit

This might seem the most obvious quality of a wine's taste. But fruit is the starting-point of wine, the substance it is made from. Thus to say that a wine is fruity is to suggest that it has gone through all the processes which have transformed it from uninteresting grapes into a miraculous drink, for nothing.

'Fruity' should be the bluffer's last resort. 'Grapey' is a somewhat different matter, because only wines made from certain kinds of grape, especially Muscat, actually taste, or should taste of grapes.

Body

This is an essential description. Unlike women, wines generally aspire to be **full-bodied**. Wines with insufficient body are said to be 'thin', which is not a compliment. On the other hand, wines with too much body can be called 'fat', which is slightly insulting. Male wine people, particularly after a glass or two,

21

are prone to talk of wine in female terms (especially the Germans) thus: 'This is the beautiful girl you take to the Opera ...and this is the woman you marry.'

There are, of course, all kinds of other approaches to talking about the taste of wine. There is some famous advice to be 'boldly meaningless' and talk about 'cornery wines' and other such things. You can always try long German words. Then there is the *Brideshead Revisited* style, abominably precious ('Shy, like a gazelle') but possibly due for resuscitation.

At the other extreme there is the blunt Antipodean approach prevalent down under, such as 'Not a wine to wrap around your tonsils.'

Finally, there is one all-embracing term you can offer, and that is **pronounced**. "This wine has a pronounced bouquet, don't you think?" is a comment which is both safe and more or less meaningless which is what the bluffer is aiming at, after all.

Great Vintages of the Past

Vintages are like 18th century battles. The French win most of them, the Germans put in the occasional brilliant victory, and the Italians don't try.

It could be impressive though probably completely useless, to be able to reel off a few of the great years of the past:

• The year of Halley's comet, 1811, and the year of Revolutions, 1848, are two quite easy ones to remember (probably easier to remember than to drink).

- Then 1870 (the clarets of that year took 80 years to come round, which must have been mortifying for the original purchasers), and the great pair of 1899 and 1900.

- Good vintages quite often come in pairs: 1928 and 1929, 1961 and 1962, 1970 and 1971, and 1982 and 1983, 1985 and 1986.

- On the other hand, good vintages also come singly: 1945, 1959, 1966. Or in trios: 1947, 1948,1949; 1988, 1989, 1990.

There are several things to note here:

a) that when talking about great vintages people always seem to mean great *claret* vintages.

b) that great claret vintages now come on average about two years out of three.

c) that vintages of the century occur at least twice a decade.

If someone says, 'Of course, 1928, was a wonderful vintage for claret,' you can try retorting, "Yes, but very poor for Tokay" or "Yes, but a freak rainstorm practically destroyed the vintage in the Barossa valley." It is highly unlikely the other person will know anything about old vintages in obscure areas.

BUYING WINE

Impulse buying of wine, as with cars, is invariably fatal. Prepare for buying by deciding whether you want wine for drinking with an appreciative friend, a dinner party, for immediate consumption or for laying down. Next, decide what price per bottle you can afford for your purposes and stick to it.

You have four options as to where to buy:

Supermarkets

These have forced themselves into first position by their sheer size and muscle power. They have obvious advantages: you can buy lettuce and Château Lafite (well, almost) at one and the same time. Because they are so big they can sell more cheaply – but they are also very good at convincing you they are less expensive than anywhere else when this is not necessarily the case. More to the point, they have good ranges of wine. But they also have a serious disadvantage: if you do find a nice wine in a supermarket and serve it to your friends, there is every chance they will know exactly where it comes from and exactly how much it costs. 'This Château Bon Marche of yours is very nice: much nicer than the one I bought last week.'

Specialist Wine Merchants and Shops

These are likely to be smaller and friendlier. They may even have people in them who know something about wine.You need to be careful however, especially when entering the most salubrious such as Berry Bros. and Justerini and Brooks in London. Those who work in them have all been to public schools and wear pinstripe shirts and tend to expect similar standards from their customers. However, some of the most dynamic and imaginative wine merchants operate in the country. You should know of at least one of these (e.g. Adnams, Alex Findlater, Lay & Wheeler, Laymont & Shaw, La Vigneronne for wines from Alsace and rarities): they have both the best lists and, because competition in the wine trade is now so hot, often the best prices too.

Wine Warehouses

These sprang into prominence because they had a 'real', functional appeal, like places to eat called kitchens or granaries – the idea being that you are cutting out the smooth middleman and getting the product, with a few rough edges, at source. But warehouses are not warehouses at all, just retail outlets like anywhere else. On other hand, some of them do sell excellent wines very cheaply (Bibendum, Majestic and Winecellars are three of the best). They also do the very sensible thing of allowing you to taste wines before buying. With very inexpensive wines you will say that this is not merely an advantage, it is a necessity.

Off-licences and High Street Chains

These used to come bottom of the list. They are still the source of most of the dreaded double-litres of Valpolicella which give unpleasant post-prandial effects.

Their prices are often scandalous. It is unusual to see bottles properly stored in them. The people who run them tend to own savage Alsatian dogs which guard the till. However, up-market chains (such as Bottoms Up and Wine Rack) have done much to reverse the old image. And chains do have one advantage: they open at the times you need them most, except on Sunday afternoons.

Wine Society

The Wine Society will deliver free to any location in mainland Britain, and so it is highly recommended to those who live in Pembrokeshire, Cornwall, the Scottish Highlands and other extremities which decent wine doesn't normally reach. The delivery charge is built into the prices, so it is not recommended to those living within easy access of wine outlets.

Wine at Auction

People have romantic ideas about auctions. The eagle-eyed auctioneer with his hammer and superhumanly quick reactions; the cryptic gestures, the fear of involuntarily raising an eyebrow and landing oneself with an old master; the eternal hope of discovering a bargain: in the case of wine at auction, most of these ideas should be abandoned.

A lot of wine finds its way to the auction rooms as a last resort, or, quite simply, because it has gone off. There are bargains to be had as well, but it is a high-risk area and you are earnestly advised to taste before buying. Christie's South Kensington and other auction houses hold regular pre-sale tastings. If you wish for a free glass there is no point in arriving more than half an hour after the starting time – they tend to fill up with free-loaders. Disgraceful really; some people do anything for a glass or two.

Understanding the Label

There is one further obstacle in the path of appreciating wine, that of deciphering the sometimes arcane and confusing information printed on the label. The worst offenders here are undoubtedly the Germans, who compound the sin of overcomplicating their wine nomenclature with the use of unreadable Gothic types. If you can understand a German wine label, you can understand anything. For instance:

German imperial eagle – possible fascist tendencies

NAHE – it comes from the Nahe region

1976er – easy: the vintage

Niederhäuser – it comes from a small town called Niederhausen

Hermannmunster – it comes from a vineyard called Hermannmunster in that town

Riesling – it is made from the Riesling grape

Auslese – it is made from selected, late gathered grapes

Qualitätswein Mit Prädikat – it is a quality wine (i.e. made with grapes) and it has a title

Amtliche Prüfungsnummer 1 750 053/51/77 – totally irrelevant

Verwaltung der Staatliche Weinbaudomänen Niederhauesen-Schlossböckelheim – the grower

e – mysterious letter: something to do with the EC

0.71 – only contains 70 cl., not 75, damnit.

If German wine labels contain too much information (and they do), others contain too little. Greek wines are particular offenders: not only named after Greek gods (Aphrodite, Bacchus), tragic heroes (Othello, Orestes) or, mystifyingly, lavatory cleansers (Demestica), their labels tell you nothing about the vintage, region or anything else you want to know. On the other hand given the quality of most Greek wines, this may be a sensible policy.

In general, things to look out for on labels (so as to hold forth in the appropriate direction) are:

The vintage – This is usually clearly visible. Some wines are non-vintage, but you know that the only acceptable non-vintage wines are sherry (which never has a vintage), and champagne.

The grape variety – Don't expect this in all cases. The aristocratic wines (claret and burgundy, for instance) do not specify their grape variety: you are expected to know it.

The country of origin – Always look out for this: some bottles carry the mark of shame 'EC Tafelwein'. This means they have been dredged up from the Community Wine Lake and bottled by bureaucrats.

The region – Look out for words like A.C., D.O.C., etc. which tell you the wine comes from a designated area. With Italian wines this is mostly a bad thing.

Bottling information – Whether the wine has been bottled at the Château (always considered a good thing), or estate, in the country of origin, or in England (always considered a bad thing).

WINE AROUND THE WORLD

There are more than 4,000 named varieties of the domesticated vine. Don't panic. It would be a bold person who claimed to be able to distinguish more than 30 by taste, and for practical purposes you will be able to get by with less than a dozen.

1. Cabernet Sauvignon

The most famous red Bordeaux grape, now also grown in California, Australia, Spain, Italy, Bulgaria, etc. It has in fact become the world's No.1 grape. This could be because wines made from it taste rather like Ribena. They also taste roughly the same wherever the grape is grown, which is useful as you know what you'll get.

2. Chardonnay

The grape used to make white burgundy, and (with two red ones) champagne. It, too, is grown successfully in California, Australia, Spain, Italy, Bulgaria, etc. The world's No. 1 white grape, it also tends to taste roughly the same wherever it is grown.

3. Chenin Blanc

White grape grown in the Loire valley and also in South Africa probably the most revolting grape variety in the world, it generally produces wines which smell and taste of vomit. In favoured corners of the Loire it does somehow manage to come up with some of the best dry and sweet wines in the world. In less favoured corners it produces a lot of ordinary sparkling wine.

4. Gewurztraminer

(Also known as Traminer, but that was apparently too short and easy to pronounce.) This grape imparts a very pronounced, supposedly spicy aroma and rich flavour. You either love it or hate it.

5. Merlot

The other red Bordeaux grape, also grown in California, Italy, Bulgaria, etc. It often makes more palatable wines than Cabernet Sauvignon, less tough and tannic, but it is deemed to be not as good, possibly because wines made from it *don't* taste of Ribena.

6. Pinot Noir

Red grape of notoriously difficult, temperamental character. An artistic type, which like, Solzhenitsyn, Ovid and Oscar Wilde goes into a decline when exiled, in this case from its native lands of Burgundy and Champagne.

7. Riesling

The most important thing is to pronounce it properly, 'Reezling' not 'Ryezling'. the next most important thing is to be aware that a lot of so-called Riesling, e.g. Welsch Riesling, grown confusingly in Czechoslovakia and the Lutomer Riesling, is not real Riesling at all.

The true Riesling is the best German grape and makes rather tart wines which you may correctly call 'steely'. When they get older, you call them 'petrolly', after the little known variant called Diesling which is used to fuel taxis.

8. **Sauvignon Blanc**

Fashionable white grape variety, it is pretty tart and supposed to impart the smell of crushed nettles. This is the grape that is used to make Sancerre and Pouilly Fumé, which is why in California (where they grow it, like everything else) it is called Fumé Blanc.

9. **Sémillon**

Possibly the world's most undervalued white grape The noble rot (see Glossary) likes to attack it, especially in Sauternes. The Australians are going for it in a big way as well, and it seems to thrive on it.

10. **Syrah**

Possibly the world's most undervalued red grape, used to make the great northern Rhône wines. The Aussies like this one as well, but call it Shiraz, which sounds better if said in Australian.

Other grape varieties to look out for are:

Gamay – a purple grape used to make Baujolais, but strangely not much else.

Muscadet – a grape variety which gives its name to a wine and doesn't taste of anything much; not to be confused with

Muscat – a grape which *does* impart a very strong taste (of Muscat) and which is itself not to be confused with Oman, not a grape variety at all.

For really obscure varieties, try the French Viognier (only used to make Condrieu and Château Grillet), the Catalan Xarel-lo with its unique hyphenated double 'l', and the German Ortega (also grown in England) named after the Spanish philosopher Ortega y Gasset. Nobody knows why.

France

France is an overrated area, so you can get considerable mileage from the line that:

a) France has been resting on her laurels for far too long;

b) her wines are made from underripe grapes, and

c) better value for money can be obtained elsewhere.

However, this gambit does need to be backed up by skeletal knowledge of the major French wine regions, because however much you try to criticise it (and do so, vigorously), France remains the No.1 wine country and the one everyone else tries to imitate.

You can start by claiming that the most exciting and best-value wines in France come from the less well-known areas – i.e:

French Country Wines

Enthuse over the up-and-coming appellations of the once despised Midi-Corbières and Minervois especially, and Côtes de Rousillon, but not Fitou. Say you find

Madiran more interesting than Cahors (famous for its black wine which, of course, is not black), and Vin de pays des Côtes de Gascogne (made from grapes surplus to requirements for Armagnac) infinitely preferable to Muscadet.

Other obscure country wines to enthuse over are:

- Pacherenc du Vic-Bilh [pronounced 'pasherank dew vikbee'], just the name will score points;

- Bandol (the only distinguished wine of the Côte d'Azur);

- Irouléguy, the wine of the French Basque country, and

- the Chardonnays of Limoux, previously only known for the would-be-Champagne sparkler, Blanquette de Limoux.

Bordeaux

Bordeaux should be greeted with a wry chuckle. The best Bordeaux wines have become far too expensive to drink (their appeal turned into investment commodities). However, their value as an investment depends upon their being drunk (so that they become progressively more rare) and as they are currently being hoarded, there is a fair chance that the prices will topple. On the other hand people have been predicting this for a long time: the last occasion it happened was 1974.

In the meantime there are a few facts you should

know. Bordeaux is one of the Englishman's wines and as such is known (for no good reason) as **claret**. The English owned Bordeaux for much of the Middle Ages and the great château wines were developed for the British market in the 17th century. The French are notoriously ignorant about claret.

Bordeaux (claret) is the most aristocratic of all wines. In 1855 the Bordeaux châteaux were divided into a system of 1st, 2nd, 3rd, 4th and 5th classed growths. Few are malignant, but you should argue that the classification is absurdly outdated. Say that the bourgeois growths such as Chasse-Spleen, Poujeaux and Pibran are infinitely better than many classed growths. Produce a little-known château from one of the Bordeaux satellite areas such as Bourg, Blaye or Côtes de Castillon and say it is just as good as many famous names.

(Note the 'many', which does not commit you to dismissing them all.) It may not be, but it will certainly be one you can afford.

Burgundy

Two approaches are possible here.

The first is an even more contemptuous chuckle than that with which you greeted Bordeaux: "The Burgundians are living in the Middle Ages. The weather is atrocious, the wine-making techniques often faulty, the subdivision of properties a joke, the prices a scandal. Few people are gullible enough to buy most burgundy."

The second approach is more indulgent. "Yes, Burgundy is impossibly complicated, and the wines usually overpriced. But it is *so* rewarding. When you track down that obscure, perfect bottle, the pleasure is incomparable."

Take your pick, but if you choose the latter, you will need to know some names. The line with burgundy is that the *grower* is all-important. Dismiss the big merchant houses (négociants) with the exception of Jadot, Jaffelin, Louis Latour (whites only) and Joseph Drouhin. Name the smart small négociants, Olivier Leflaive (son of the most famous grower of white burgundy) and Chartron et Trebuchet.

The Romanée-Conti estate is the most famous among small growers, not least because of its high priced wines, and thus an excellent one to mention. So is the name of the most respected small grower, now retired, Henri Jayer.

Jean Grivot is one which has employed the controversial Lebanese oenologist (the wine professional's professional) Guy Accad. You do not need to know anything about Accad or his methods just express approval or disapproval.

Alsace

Here you must always refer to the wines as 'from Alsace' for, as the great wine writer André Simon once remarked, 'Alsatian is ze dog'. And many German wine growers would agree. Alsace has great difficulty deciding whether it is French or German (it has now decided to be French, but it is difficult to believe this when they still speak German and eat sauerkraut): the wines reflect this schizophrenia.

They taste half-German (grapey) and half-french (dry). Some people find this unacceptable and think they should make up their minds. But you could say it gives the best of both worlds.

The first thing to get straight about wines from Alsace is that they are named after grape varieties, e.g. Riesling, Gewurztraminer, etc. You are best to avoid the latter (too obvious, even an ignoramus can detect it in blind tastings) and praise the Tokay-Pinot-Gris (much more subtle) instead (which you know has nothing to do with the Hungarian Tokay or the Italian Tocai. Another smart, upwardly mobile grape variety to enjoy is Pinot Blanc, in preference to the popular Sylvaner, which is now on the wane.

As with other regions of France, the names of négociants (make an exception for Trimbach's top Riesling, Clos Sainte Hune) are outflanked by the growers. Drool over Zind-Humbrech's Tokay-Pinot-Gris from the Rangen at Thann, Riesling from the Brand and Gewurztraminer from the Goldert.

Other growers to be openly admired include André Ostertag who uses new oak (a hint of vanilla), and Marc Kreydenweiss from the unfashionable north.

The Loire

Of the Loire there is a good argument for sticking to the châteaux and forgetting the wines, which are noted mainly for their unrelentingly high acidity. They also tend to be made from the repellent Chenin Blanc grape. Two exceptions are Muscadet and Sancerre. One of the best-kept secrets in wine is that Muscadet does not taste of anything to speak of (it is extremely hard to identify in blind tastings). Sancerre and its neighbour, Pouilly-Fumé, on the other hand, are the easiest to identify by taste.

It is a good idea to overlook these popular names. They are, in any case, not the best Loire wines, which you know to be the dry Savennières and Vouvray and the sweet Bonnezeaux [pronounced 'bonzo'] and Quarts de Chaume ['cardeshowm']. The last two are much better than the well-publicised Moulin Touchais and very few people have heard of them. They are absurdly good value as a result.

There is also some good bluffing potential to be had from the red wines of the Loire. The best of these is Bourgeuil, difficult to say and not be mixed up with Bourgogne or Bourg, a small town near Bordeaux. It is made from the Cabernet Franc grape and is about as close to Ribena as you can get without infringing the patent.

The vintage should usually be the latest or the one before that. Conversely, with the sweet wines, the older the better.

The Rhône

As Rhône wines are mainly red you need not worry at all about the whites, which are either very rare and expensive e.g. Condrieu, Château Grillet, or not as good as the red equivalent.

The best northern Rhône wine is Hermitage. It used to be added to Château Lafite in the last century: since Hermitage is too strong to drink on its own and Château Lafite often too weak, it made very good sense. This wouldn't be allowed these days, of course.

The best Hermitage grower is agreed to be Gérard Chave ("Marvellous wine, bit of an eccentric fellow, though"). Crozes-Hermitage ['crows-airmitaj'] is a less strong, less expensive form of Hermitage. The growers and shippers Paul Jaboulet Aîné do a very good one called Domaine de Thalabert.

Côte Rôtie is the other prized northern Rhône wine. You can try saying it's better than Hermitage, if you like. The grower to mention here is Marcel Guigal.

The southern Rhône is simpler still. There is only one really famous wine, the strong red Château Neuf-du-Pape. Once upon a time this was dubious stuff. Its reputation went through a slump, not surprisingly, but it is now definitely on the up. A good ploy is to mention white Château Neuf-du-Pape, almost unheard of until very recently.

Conversely, with the other well-known southern Rhône wine, Beaumes de Venise, the thing to do is enthuse over the little-known red rather than the delectable, over-exposed honey-sweet white. With any luck, the non-bluffer will not know that the red can be bought for much less. It is in fact a straight-forward Côtes du Rhônes, but not to be scorned. Say that, 'in its class' it is far better value than Beaujolais.

The Rhône also produces Tavel, one of the very few rosés about which it is permissible to be polite.

Vintages: A convenient, but unfortunately not entirely true theory, is that since the Rhône is so far south, vintages do not matter. Another theory, also not true, is that good vintages in the north are not good in the south. 1988 and 1990 are both excellent, and you should say so.

Beaujolais and Mâconnais

These regions are a southern extension of Burgundy and make some attractive red and white wines. It is a pity, therefore, that the wine everybody associates the region is the generally unpleasant purple beverage, Beaujolais Nouveau. You can make the point that it is hardly surprising Beaujolais Nouveau is unpleasant since it is expressly designed to be:

a) drunk far too young

b) transported from France in various unsuitable ways (fast cars, helicopters, pipelines) for publicity purposes.

Bluffers should only ever proffer a Beaujolais Nouveau which is at least five years old, lightly dismissing anything younger as nonsense or simply skilful sales talk.

The Beaujolais to praise are the little-known village wines or **crus**. Fleurie and Moulin-a-Vent, fashionable mainly because they are relatively pronounceable; Brouilly and Côte de Brouilly (which are often just as good) because they are not.

The white Mâcon wines are the nearest non-millionaires can get to white burgundy. The most famous of them, Pouilly-Fuissé, (nothing to do with Pouilly-Fumé) is not worth bothering about because:

a) it is grossly over-priced

b) it is all shipped to America anyway.

Plain Mâcon-Villages is perhaps a little obvious (it can even be found on Chinese restaurant wine lists), but you would do well to mug up some of the individual village names, which are memorably odd, e.g. Mâcon-Lugny [pronounced 'loony'] and Mâcon-Prissé. Louis Latour have a good Mâcon-Lugny, Les Genièvres, and Duboeuf have delightful Mâcon wines too, such as Mâcon-Villages from the Lenoir estate.

Vintages: Like Burgundy, only less important, is the general rule. 1985 was hailed as the best Beaujolais vintage for fifty years. The same happened with 1988, 1989 and 1990.

Germany

It may surprise some people who know that Germany produces bland sugary wines one step up from fruit juice, that this country can also produce some of the world's greatest, most individual wines. They are constantly developing new methods, new grape varieties and new clones of existing varieties which produce higher and higher yields – up to five times as great as in less technically-minded Spain. The result is mainly millions and millions of gallons of Liebfraumilch, which all tastes roughly the same.

But there is another side to the German wine industry in which technical skill is put at the service of individuality, sometimes to an almost absurd degree. Up to twenty different wines can be made and marketed from one small patch of vineyard.

One problem is that most of the best German wines are sweet. But you must not fall into the philistine trap of condemning all sweet wines. Puddings, patisserie and fruits are sweet, so why shouldn't some wines be the equivalent of the dessert rather than the main course? Meanwhile the Germans have started to make a lot of their wines dry (trocken) or half-dry (halb-trocken): these take a bit of getting used to, but go well with food. They are an excellent bluffing area because few people seem to be aware of their existence.

The German system of wine classification is so obsessively logical as to be completely mystifying. Wines are classified first according to where they come from. This may sound sensible enough, but it does not just refer to an area (e.g. Mosel-Saar-Ruwer, Rheingau) but, often, an individual vineyard in a minute village, e.g. Niederwallufer Blankenberg. Words ending -er are usually villages e.g. Forster = from Forst. But some words ending -er are vineyards, e.g. Forster Ungeheuer.

You can have some fun confounding an audience with: "And how about this for logic: there are two wines, one called Zeltinger Sonnenuhr, the other Zeltinger Muntzlay. Both come from the village of Zeltingen in the Mosel? Right. One comes from the Sonnenuhr vineyard and the other from the Muntzlay vineyard? Wrong: one comes from the Sonnenuhr vineyard but the other can come from any vineyard in the Zeltingen district."

German quality wines are also classified according to the degree of sweetness or ripeness of the grapes from which they are made:

- QbA (Qualitätswein bestimmte Anbaugebiete) the lowest quality grade, which can be sweetened with extra sugar during fermentation;

- Kabinett, riper than QbA but often not so sweet;

- Spätlese [pronounced 'shpat-e-laser'], riper and usually sweeter than Kabinett;

and so on through Auslese and Beerenauslese up to Trockenbeerenauslese, which may sound dry (trocken), but is in fact intensely sweet, being made from individually picked grapes shrivelled with the noble rot. You will pay the same as a good seat at Covent Garden Opera house per bottle for this doubtful privilege.

There is also Eiswein ['icevine'] which is not a wine that you put in the freezer but one made from frozen grapes picked and crushed while still frozen. The people who make Eiswein get pretty frozen too.

The Germans are great ones for inventing new grape varieties. But having invented hundreds of them with peculiar names like Huxelrebe and Optima, they now seem to be deciding that Riesling was the best all along. The only new crossing whose name you really need to know is Müller-Thurgau because it is the most widely planted grape in Germany. It makes wines which are quick to mature and easy to forget.

A couple of good, traditional grape varieties are Sylvaner (which makes the best wine in Franconia) and Rulander.

Because they have made their classification system so absurdly complicated, the Germans find their quality wines very difficult to sell, so the lovely fresh and delicate wines of the Mosel-Saar-Ruwer, the more full-bodied Rheingaus and the sometimes luscious Palatinate wines are often delightfully inexpensive.

Growers are crucial in Germany, as they are in Alsace and Burgundy. Some good names to bandy about are:

J. J. Prüm – A semi-legendary figure who refuses to sell his wine either before he considers it ready or to people he considers unworthy.

Friedrich-Wilhelm-Gymnasium – The school that Karl Marx went to in Trier, which also owns some very good vineyards.

Schloss Vollrads – A famous old castle in the Rheingau, owned by a very tall man with a very long name, Count Matuschka-Greiffenklau.

The Three B's (**Bassermann-Jordan**, **von Buhl** and **Bürklin-Wolf**) – The three biggest estates in the Palatinate region.

Vintages: Very good vintages, with enough sun to ripen the grapes, are rare in Germany. 1983, 1976 and 1971 are the best recent ones. However, wines made in less good vintages can, after ten, twenty or even fifty years, taste quite delicious too. So hang on to yours.

Italy

Italy used to be safe to regard as a joke, being the source of much dubious, unpleasant and from time to time, poisonous wine. Now, however, it is the fastest-improving wine country, and therefore one with maximum bluffing potential. Start by saying that all Italian wine laws are more honoured in the breach than the observance.

The best Italian wines, such as the Cabernet

Sauvignon-based Sassicaia, and the so-called Super Tuscans pioneered by Antinori's Tignanello only qualify for the lowest category of vino da taola. (But argue that 100 per cent Sangiovese wines such as Castello di Volpaia's Coltassala and Isole e Olena's Cepparello are superior.)

Barolo and Barbaresco, the lumbering red giants of Piedmont, are controversial. Be bold: declare that Angelo Gaja, the superstar of Barbaresco (and of Barolo) uses too much new oak: and that traditionalists such as Aldo Conterno and Mauro Mascarello are to be preferred. Extol the virtues of the little-known white varietals of Piedmont, Arneis and Favorita, but reject Gavi for being (like most Italian whites) more popular than they deserve to be.

Soave and Valpolicella are two of the most abused wine names in the world, and a good ruse is to comment on how much these have improved: praise the Soaves of Pieropan (especially the sweet Recioto) and Anselmi, and the incomparable Valpolicella of Giuseppe Quintarelli.

You can also gain valuable points by claiming that Marsala is unjustly neglected, and that Marco de Bartoli's Vecchio Sampri is the best alternative to amontillado sherry.

Spain and Portugal

Spain used to be known mainly for sherry and port but increasingly appreciated as sources of good value table wines, especially Rioja ['ree-och-are'] with its mellow oaky reds. (These are supposed to be matured in oak barrels but bags of oak shavings suspended in the wine, some claim, has the same effect.)

Now that Rioja has became so popular and pricey you need to assert your preference for the lesser known: state that the best Rioja reservas and gran reservas (from companies such as La Rioja Alta and Beronia) are unfairly neglected and wonderful value, and that 'given a choice' you would select the single-vineyard Rioja (very few of which exist so it is comparatively simple to remember the names): Remelluri, Contino and Marques de Murrieta are the ones to go for.

But Rioja is not the only Spanish wine to admire. Penedés in Catalonia is the home of Miguel Torres (praise especially the single-vineyard Mas La Plana Cabernet Sauvignon and Milmanda Chardonnay), Jean Leon (a Los Angeles restaurateur turned wine-maker) and Raimat. The most famous and expensive Spanish wine, Vega Sicilia, is over-oaked and over-priced, so rather support the new star, also from Ribera del Duero, Pesquera.

Portugal is more problematic, partly because of the stubborn Portuguese adherence to funny old Portuguese grape varieties, but also because of pre-historic wine-making techniques (leaving wines in old oak barrels until they taste of little but acorns). Names to mention are Bairrada [pronounced appropriately 'buy harder'] and single-vineyard vinho verde [pronounced 'vaird'].

Eastern Europe

Bulgarian Cabernet Sauvignon no longer has the advantage of novelty, neither is it the most reasonable wine on the shelf. Changes in the country's political system make its future uncertain, and while awaiting further developments, you can praise Bulgarian Merlot and the native Bulgarian variety Mavrud. Express a preference for Saka Mountain Cabernet over the basic kind from Suhindol.

Show your approval of Romanian Pinot Noir and the extraordinary dessert wines of the Crimea such as Massandra. Hungary has gone determinedly capitalist and privatised the grand old imperialist dessert wine, Tokay. Few Russian table wines have yet penetrated western European defences. Some are heavily built and awesomely destructive.

Australia

Australian wines must be mentioned before Californian. Wines like Rosemount Roxburgh Chardonnay and Wynn's Coonawarra Cabernet Sauvignon are being ordered at the most important tables in the world.

Once upon a time the only Australian regions you needed to know about were the Barossa valley near Adelaide and the Hunter valley north of Sydney, with the occasional vineyard from Victoria. Things are now much more complicated – which is not such a bad thing since both the Barossa and the Hunter are in theory (though not in practice) too hot to make great wine. Cool climate vineyards are all the rage in Australia, quite a contrast to Europe where so many wine growers have difficulties getting the grapes to ripen at all.

Cool climate regions to champion are:

- Margaret River in Western Australia, which is not a river, shows no sign of Margaret, and is not at all cool (wineries to support here are Leeuwin for Chardonnay and Moss Wood for everything)

- the Adelaide Hills (home of Brian Croser's Petaluma and Adam Wynn's Mountadam), and

- Coonawarra in remote South Australia.

Cool climate mania has reached crazy extremes in Tasmania and the bungaloid outskirts of Melbourne, where Garry Crittenden makes Cabernet Sauvignon as unripe as that of Bordeaux in a moderate vintage, and just as effective.

Good bluffing gambits are the sweet liqueur muscats of north-east Victoria, which after decades of ageing achieve the consistency and taste of black treacle. Other Australian fortified wines, especially the splendid old ports made by Seppelts in the Barossa are equally well worth supporting.

California

The Californians have approached wine-making with the same manic enthusiasm which they devote to fitness, cuisine and sex. The results have had the same tendency to be larger and glossier than life, but they are now getting better at imitating the subtleties of European wines. Indeed, you should argue that California has gone too far in the direction of so-called 'elegance': Chardonnays, far from the buttery, buxom lovelies of the early 1980s, have tried to imitate anorexic Chablis, and Cabernet Sauvignons have become light and insipid. Yearn for a return to the big blockbuster styles of yesteryear.

Names are a problem in California, because there are so many of them (the rabbit-like propagation of boutique wineries is becoming a menace) and they are always changing. However, there are a few constant stars. Robert Mondavi continues to be innovative and brilliant: say that his Pinot Noir Reserve is now better even than his Cabernet Sauvignon (and far better than anything from Oregon).

Indeed, proclaim that Californian Pinot Noir is infinitely more exciting than Californian Cabernet and cite Saintsbury, Calera and Au Bon Climat as proof. Or claim that Syrah is now more exciting than Pinot Noir – Qupé and Randall Grahm's whacky Bonny Doon being the key names. Joseph Phelps is reliable. Clos du Val, run by the Frenchman Bernard Portet, is a touchstone for classy Cabernet Sauvignon. In the Napa valley, hillside vineyards are the current concept: Randy Dunn's Cabernet Sauvignon from Howell Mountain and Peter Newton's from Spring Mountain are two of the finest.

It is also possible to impress by the gentle suggestion that Napa is over exposed and better value is to be found in superb Sonoma district – Clos du Bois and Benziger Estate are the names to favour.

New Zealand

New Zealand has a reputation based on its brilliant grassy, nettley, gooseberry-tasting Sauvignon Blanc. The leader in this wine is the excellent Cloudy Bay, devised by David Hohnen of Cape Mentelle in

Western Australia and made by Kevin Judd. But you can score points by pointing out:

a) that it is at its best in the first year, after which it loses its freshness and appeal (the perfect excuse for needing to consume it immediately)

b) the Chardonnay is even better.

Chile

Tipped by many as the emerging wine country of the 1990s, Chile has the classic French grape varieties (Cabernet Sauvignon, Chardonnay, Sauvignon Blanc, Pinot Noir) producing wines of the highest quality.

The new-style, fashion-conscious Chilean wineries such as Santa Rita are ashamed of the continuing use of vats made of the Chilean wood called raulí, but you should enthuse over the special bitter-tobacco flavour that maturation in these vats gives to old-fashioned wines like Cousiño Macul's Antiguas Reservas Cabernet.

There are two things to point out about Chile; first its wine industry goes back to the 1540s. Second, Chile's vineyards have never been affected by *phylloxera* (see History) because the destructive little vine aphid was, quite simply, unable to cross the Andes.

WINING AND DINING

It is important to remember that restaurants make most of their profits from wine, and it is not uncommon to find mark-ups of between 300 and 400 per cent. The situation is even worse in France, where an already punitive duty pushes the price of ordinary wine out of the reach of those who need it most. But a mark-up of 100 per cent is considered almost a minimum anywhere and that can hardly be described as generous.

Some restaurants get away with scandalous prices: people fork out double the average high street price for the most basic plonk in unexceptional brasseries without demur. It is depressing to behold. Bear in mind that this wine, often of the most dubious provenance, probably cost the producer the equivalent of a box of matches to make, and even with shipping and duty and a reasonable profit margin for the grower and merchant, can hardly cost the restaurant more than the price of a packet of cigarettes.

When going to a licensed restaurant be aware that you are letting yourself in for an elaborate ritual. Wine waiters are taught to go through various motions, handing the wine list to the most important person, pouring out a little for him or her to taste, but they are rarely taught the purpose of these motions.

For this reason, and because most people are so extraordinarily deferential, wine waiters do not take at all kindly to having their wines sent back. A few simple rules may help you to hold your own:

1. Be polite but above all firm. Any trace of hesitancy plays right into the hands of the waiter, who invariably thinks the customer is either stupid,

wrong or trying it on.

2. Send the wine back immediately after the waiter has given you a small amount to taste. If you delay, and start drinking, the waiter will understandably assume:

   a) that you are unsure of your ground

   b) that the wine is drinkable.

3. Only claim to be a wine writer or expert as a last resort and if you are wearing a suit. For some reason waiters do not believe that casually dressed people can know anything about wine.

Of course, this kind of heavy-handed tactic should not be necessary. It can ruin a romantic evening. On the other hand it may also be a good test. A partner who will not allow you to challenge a wine waiter may not be prepared to give you much leeway in other areas.

You should be aware that it is quite rare to be given the right wine in a restaurant in the first place. One vintner, an excessively honest character, sent back a wine which was in fact superior to the one he had ordered only to be told by the waiter that the bottle he had been given in error was 'vairy nice wine, come in fresh today'.

Waiter, This Wine is Corked

It is widely believed that in order to qualify as a real wine expert you need to be able to tell instantly whether or not a wine is corked. In fact no wine term is attended by so much confusion.

Some people, in their innocence, believe that a corked wine has bits of cork floating around in it: this is not the case. Bits of cork, though unsightly, in no way affect the taste of wine. If they did, every bottle would be corked, since the wine inside is constantly in contact with the cork.

Some quite knowledgeable people say that a corked wine tastes of cork. But as not many of us chew cork for fun, it is easier to recognise as wine which smells musty and dank, like a house with rising damp. On the other hand since even experts seem unable to agree on the exact definition, you might take the line that the word 'corked' is strictly meaningless. Declare that, as no-one really knows what it means, it is much more honest to use the term 'off' – a term quite anathema to the wine expert.

There are various kinds of 'off-ness'. Apart from the dank musty odour, there is oxidation. This is what happens when wine is exposed to the atmosphere. It ends up going brown and smelling a bit like toffee. With some wines, especially sherry and madeira, this is actually considered desirable, and the word 'maderised' (i.e. tasting like madeira) is a good term to master and employ when faced with any wine which is tired, old or has been sitting around for far too long. Could be used of some people, come to that.

Additives and Adulterations

Wine-makers committing illegal adulteration have been much in the news. First there was anti-freeze (known to bluffers as diethylene glycol), which made wine taste fuller and richer, and did not actually kill anybody, but is poisonous in large doses. So is wine, in really large doses. The bluffer, on that basis, could always try defending anti-freeze.

The second was methanol, which is poisonous in very small doses. It killed quite a number of people, so should probably not be defended.

As a result of these scandals, people started to worry about other substances which are regularly added to wine. These include cultured yeasts (used in Australia), sugar beet, sulphur dioxide, tartaric acid, mud, egg whites, pine resin, dried ox blood and the shredded swim-bladder of the sturgeon. Most of these things are not just harmless but positively beneficial. Point out that people have tried making organic wine, but it tends to taste of manure.

There are a few treatments of wine which can be justifiably condemned. Filtering through asbestos is probably undesirable, and indeed excessive filtering and centrifuging are now considered a bad thing.

If you ever find funny little crystals in the bottom of the glass or bottle, remain calm, smile appreciatively and comment, "Ah, Wienstein – one doesn't see it often enough these days. A sure sign that the wine hasn't been messed about too much." These are tartaric crystals, and are a good thing. Other people may not be convinced, but they should at least be impressed.

Wine and Food

Most wine, of course, cries out to be drunk with food. It is obvious that a fine red burgundy, or Californian Cabernet was not made to be drunk on its own. The same is true of the more alcoholic white wines like white burgundy or Sauternes. But some lighter wines, mainly white but occasionally red, are actually more suited for unaccompanied consumption.

The Bach solo violin partitas of the wine world are the great Rieslings of the Mosel-Saar-Ruwer. The Maximin Grunhaus wines of Von Schubert, for instance, are too delicate and fine to have intercourse with any food. The dry Muscats of Alsace are also best drunk as an aperitif. The sweeter German wines, of Auslese standard upwards, are not really pudding wines (they don't have enough alcohol), but wines which form a dessert in themselves. One sip of Trockenbeerenauslese is probably equivalent to a whole slice of Sachertorte. And if you have to have Beaujolais Nouveau, drink it on its own, well chilled.

Funnily enough, some wines which are thought to be best drunk on their own go equally well, if not better, with food. The classic example is sherry. The heavier forms of sherry, amontillado and dry oloroso, are superb with all kinds of soups.

As to the great vexed issue of what wine goes with what food, bluffers should not feel intimidated. The golden rule is that there are *no* golden rules.

The classic axiom is that only white wine can be served with fish. It has to be admitted that most fish dishes are best accompanied by white wines, from Muscadet with shellfish to Meursault with, say, sole in a rich creamy sauce. But the Basque dish of salt cod and ratatouille is so strongly flavoured that it needs a red wine to cope with it, and some dark-fleshed fish like salmon and fresh tuna are particularly well suited to a fairly light red.

You might try some really outrageous combinations (Château Neuf with oysters perhaps, or Coquilles St. Jacques au Zinfandel) for fun – or at least claim to have tried them.

Burgundy is supposed to be the best wine with game, but you will declare that it all depends on the kind of game. A delicate partridge might be swamped by a heavy Chambertin, for instance, and an equally delicate Margaux might be just the thing. If money is no object, you are supposed to drink Château Yquem ['Ee-kem'] with foie gras.

There is also a belief that most cheeses, including the white-rinded ones like brie and camembert, are a particularly suitable accompaniment to the finest Bordeaux (claret). This is not true. White-rinded cheeses completely alter the character of fine red wines, making them taste strangely sweet. Hence the old wine trade adage, 'Sell on cheese, buy on an apple' but this only works with cheaper wines, for Château Lafite with brie is nothing like its true self and might just as well be Beaujolais.

Even cheddar can be too strong and pungent for claret. The only cheeses that go really well with fine red wine are very hard, subtly flavoured ones like the Italian pecorino and the fine Manchego cheeses from Spain. The traditional combination of port and stilton, on the other hand, can be accorded your unqualified respect.

Bluff Your Way in Sherry

Sherry is a fortified wine, like port, except that it is fortified after the fermentation has finished, and so is naturally dry. It is made in a very complicated way, like champagne: you don't need to know how this works, merely its name – the solera system.

People who know about sherry generally go for fino and manzanilla, the two driest kinds, quite delicious, but only when they are fresh. A half-empty bottle or worse still decanter, is likely to taste stale and unpleasant. These kinds of sherry should be kept in the fridge and served cold: 'Just as they serve it in those tapa bars in Jerez and Sanlucar de Barrameda.' Manzanilla, which comes from the latter town is always said to have a 'salty tang' as a result of its proximity to the Atlantic ocean. Real amontillado is splendid stuff, but increasingly difficult to find. Like most 'medium' products, it is normally far too sweet. Genuine amontillado is supposed to taste nutty.

Even more bluffing points may be scored by the mention of palo cortado and dry oloroso, now the rarest forms of sherry and excellent with soup.

Bluff Your Way in Port

Port is another of 'the Englishman's wines'. Having lost possession of Bordeaux the British needed another source of wine and Portugal, being rather a sleepy country, was happy to accommodate them. Someone with a sweet tooth then decided that Douro wine tasted nicer if its fermentation was stopped half way through with lots of grape sugar left in. Port has been made that way ever since, and Portugal doesn't seem to have changed much either. There are still a number of English colonials with names like Warre, Graham and Delaforce running around there as if nothing had happened since the 17th century. They have lunch once a week in a place called the Factory House which isn't at all like a factory, and from which foreigners and women are excluded.

The posh kind of port is vintage port. This tastes revolting until it is about 20 years old, and as a result used to be given to boys as a christening present with the idea that it would come of age at the same time as they did. The correct amount to give was a barrel or 'pipe' containing about 50 dozen bottles. Livers must have been stronger in those days: the younger Pitt, in the last week of his final illness, was restricted to one pint of port per day. Nowadays people complain of feeling delicate after a single glass.

Apart from vintage, the only other really good kind of port is old tawny, which is matured in the barrel rather than the bottle. So-called late-bottled vintage port isn't really like vintage port at all – it has no muck in the bottom, for a start. Crusted port, despite not having a vintage, is much more like the real thing (muck included). Ruby port is only suitable for drinking with lemon.

Bluff Your Way in Madeira

The odd thing about madeira is that it is the only wine to be 'boiled' – deliberately. Know that the process is called the estufa system and involves heating the wine to 120° F for a considerable length of time. This, not surprisingly, gives it a distinctive burnt flavour.

Madeira is also made from odd grape varieties Sercial, Verdelho, Bual and Malmsey, or is suppose to be. There is a rumour that these have been supplanted by a much less noble grape called Negra Tinta Mole. Certainly an awful lot of madeira is only fit for sauce. But if you give people a choice between madeira and port they always seem to choose madeira.

Bluffing with Brandy

There are a few simple rules to learn about brandy. The first is that the best brandy is made from the worst wine. The second is that brandy is supposed to get better the longer it stays in the barrel, but does not improve at all once it is in the bottle. Every year a vast amount of brandy in barrels evaporates away: in Cognac they call this the angels' share. If angels can stand young brandy they must have harder heads than us.

It is important to have an opinion on the question of Cognac versus Armagnac. Cognac is supposed to be more refined and elegant, Armagnac earthier and more robust. Take your pick, but if you are going for Cognac, try to avoid the more commercial brands like Martell, Hennessy and Courvoisier. The connoisseur's brand is Delamain Pale and Dry.

An effective ruse is to have a bottle of very cheap Spanish (Fundador) or Greek (Metaxa 7 Star) brandy in reserve. Bring it out with a flourish, and pour out a huge measure saying, "I have a kind of perverse relish for the really rough stuff – don't you? It hurts like hell, but you can *feel* it doing you good."

GLOSSARY

Appellation – Designated area of wine production protected by elaborate laws which are either ignored or irrelevant.

A.C. – Appellation controlée, which applies to French wines from designated regions of which certain standards are demanded. This does not necessarily mean that they are any good.

D.O.C. – Much the same as A.C., only Italian.

Botrytis – A fungus essential to producing really sweet, concentrated wines like Sauternes or the German Trockenbeerenauslese. Known as 'the noble rot', not to be confused with wine writer's drivel.

Bottle-sick – A temporary condition which affects wines immediately after bottling. Not the condition that affects people after drinking too many bottles.

Cap(sule) – Metal or plastic deterrent which covers the cork. Metal ones are fine, so long as they are made of lead, but there is no known aid for the tough plastic ones.

Cépage – French for grape variety.

Chaptalisation – French for the practice of adding sugar to the must, or unfermented grape juice, named after a chap called Jean Antoine Chaptal who invented it in the 18th century. The French have shrewdly decided that it sounds better than 'the practice of adding sugar.'

Château – a) in France, a castle or stately home; b) in Bordeaux, any building, outhouse, shed etc. in which, or near which, wine is made, bottled or stored.

Château-bottled – Wine which is bottled in the aforementioned building, outhouse, shed, etc.

Commune – French for parish.

Cru – French for growth. The best French wines like to call themselves grands crus (great growths), premiers crus (first growths), premiers grands crus, etc.

Extract – That which makes a wine taste nice and isn't alcohol, acidity, fruit or sugar.

Gouleyant – Excellent French word which means gulpable.

Great – Any wine or vintage which is better than average.

Fine – Ethnic term for brandy.

Marc – A kind of brandy made by distilling the skins, pips, etc. Pronounced 'Maaarrh!' Known in Italy as grappa.

M.O.G. – American for Matter Other than Grapes, e.g. "I see a little MOG has crept in here."

Oechsle – German way of measuring the ripeness of grapes. To talk about Oechsle numbers for wines ('Ah yes, 117 degrees Oechsle – phenomenal') is the equivalent of using Koechel numbers for Mozart's works; it shows you are a true pro.

Palate – Soft plate at the back of the mouth which is supposed to be an organ of taste. The palate hasn't got very much to do with taste at all, in fact. People with good palates are supposed to be skilled tasters. A good palate probably just helps you to speak distinctly.

Moelleux – French for quite sweet. Difficult word to pronounce even before drinking some.

Ordinaire – Undistinguished.

Sommelier – French for wine waiter. More or less unknown outside France.

Toffee-nosed – Description of wines which are slightly oxidised. Also applies to some wine writers.

Carafe – A wine which is meant to sound cheaper than it actually is.

Vin de table/vino da taola – Wine which will drink you under the table.

THE AUTHOR

Harry Eyres was introduced to serious wine appreciation – in the form of light Moselle – at the age of eight. He went on his first tasting trip (to Champagne and Burgundy) aged thirteen, and has never looked back since. With wine running in his blood, in both senses (his father is a wine merchant), he twice managed to carry off the coveted individual prize in the Oxford v. Cambridge Tasting Match (the bibbers' Boat race).

He went on to Christie's Wine Department, and then spent some time teaching in England and in Spain, finally deciding to become a full-time writer for the *Spectator*, the *Times* and various publishers. Between books, he returns to Spain to anaesthetise his palate with Fundador brandy in the bars of old Barcelona.

His main interests seem to be reading, writing, and drinking, not necessarily in that order.

THE BLUFFER'S GUIDES

Available at £1.99 and (new titles* £2.50) each:

Accountancy
Advertising
Antiques
Archaeology
Astrology & Fortune Telling
Ballet
Bird Watching
Bluffing
British Class
Champagne*
The Classics
Computers
Consultancy
Cricket
The European Community
Espionage
Finance
The Flight Deck
Golf
The Green Bluffer's Guide
Japan
Jazz
Journalism
Literature
Management

Marketing
Maths
Modern Art
Motoring
Music
The Occult
Opera
Paris
Philosophy
Photography
P.R.
Public Speaking
Publishing
Racing
Secretaries
Seduction
Sex
Small Business*
Teaching
Theatre
University
Weather Forecasting
Whisky
Wine
World Affairs

All these books are available at your local bookshop or newsagent, or can be ordered direct from the publisher. Prices and availability subject to change without notice. Just tick the titles you require and send a cheque or postal order (allowing in the UK for postage and packing 28p for one book and 12p for each additional book ordered) to:

Ravette Books Limited, 3 Glenside Estate, Star Road, Partridge Green, Horsham, West Sussex RH13 8RA.